# The Truth A German Atrocities

Founded on the Report of the
Committee on Alleged German Outrages

Anonymous

Alpha Editions

This edition published in 2024

ISBN : 9789362515636

Design and Setting By
**Alpha Editions**
www.alphaedis.com
Email - info@alphaedis.com

As per information held with us this book is in Public Domain.
This book is a reproduction of an important historical work. Alpha Editions uses the best technology to reproduce historical work in the same manner it was first published to preserve its original nature. Any marks or number seen are left intentionally to preserve its true form.

# Contents

INTRODUCTION. ..................................................................- 1 -
1. CIVILIANS MURDERED AND ILL-TREATED..................- 5 -
2. WOMEN MURDERED AND OUTRAGED. .......................- 18 -
3. THE MURDER AND ILL-TREATMENT OF
   CHILDREN. ......................................................................- 21 -
4. BRUTAL TREATMENT OF THE AGED, THE CRIPPLED
   AND THE INFIRM. ..........................................................- 24 -
5. THE USE OF CIVILIANS AS SCREENS. .........................- 25 -
6. THE KILLING OF WOUNDED SOLDIERS AND
   PRISONERS. ....................................................................- 27 -
7. LOOTING, BURNING AND DESTRUCTION OF
   PROPERTY. .....................................................................- 28 -
FINDINGS OF THE COMMITTEE. .........................................- 33 -

# INTRODUCTION.

*Prussia joined in a Guarantee of Belgian Neutrality.*

The neutrality of Belgium was guaranteed by a treaty signed in 1839 to which France, Prussia and Great Britain were parties.

*Recent German Assurances.*

In 1913 the German Secretary of State, at a meeting of a Budget Committee of the Reichstag, declared that "Belgian neutrality is provided for by international conventions, and Germany is determined to respect those conventions."

On July 31st, 1914, when the danger of war between Germany and France seemed imminent, Herr von Below, the German Minister in Brussels, being interrogated by the Belgian Foreign Department, replied that he knew of the assurances given by the German Chancellor in 1911 (that Germany had no intention of violating Belgian neutrality) and that he "was certain that the sentiments expressed at that time had not changed."

*Passage through Belgium Demanded by Germany.*

Nevertheless, on August 2nd, the same Minister presented a note to the Belgian Government demanding a passage through Belgium for the German Army on pain of an instant declaration of war.

*Passage Refused by Belgian King and Government.*

Startled as they were by the suddenness with which this terrific war cloud had risen on the eastern horizon, the leaders of the nation rallied round the King of Belgium in his resolution to refuse the demand and to prepare for resistance.

*Invasion.*

On the evening of August 3rd, the German troops crossed the frontier.

*Early Outbreak of Atrocities.*

No sooner had the Germans violated Belgian territory, than statements of atrocities committed by German soldiers against civilians—men, women and children—found their way into the newspapers of this country. The public could hardly believe the record of cruelty that rapidly accumulated, but the persistence with which reports from one district tallied in general outline with reports from other localities left little doubt in the public mind as to the truth of the alleged atrocities. But it became necessary to make absolutely certain of the facts.

*Home Office Collected Evidence.*

The Home Office, in the autumn of 1914, wisely decided to collect evidence of the truth, and, during the concluding months of 1914, a great number of statements taken in writing were collected from Belgian witnesses (mostly civilians), and from British officers and soldiers. The statements were taken by the staff of the Director of Public Prosecutions and a number of barristers who assisted the Home Office.

*Government Appointed a Committee to Investigate—Terms of Reference.*

On December 15th, 1914, the Government took the important step of appointing a Committee:—

> **"To consider and advise on the evidence collected on behalf of His Majesty's Government, as to outrages alleged to have been committed by German troops during the present war, cases of alleged maltreatment of civilians in the invaded territories, and breaches of the laws and established usages of war; and to prepare a report for His Majesty's Government showing the conclusion at which they arrive on the evidence now available."**

*Careful Selection of Members of Committee.*

In order that the findings of the Committee should command the confidence of the public, the Government was careful to appoint upon it men whose judicial outlook, training and experience for their responsible task could not be questioned.

> The Right Hon. VISCOUNT BRYCE, O.M., the distinguished British Ambassador at Washington from 1907 to 1912, was appointed Chairman, and the other members of the Committee were:—

> The Right Hon. SIR FREDERICK POLLOCK, Bart., who was Corpus Professor of Jurisprudence at Oxford University, 1883-1903, and is Judge of the Admiralty Court of Cinque Ports. He is one of the leading authorities on the laws of this country;

> The Right Hon. SIR EDWARD CLARKE, K.C., was Member of Parliament for Plymouth (20 years) and London City (1906); was Solicitor-General from 1886 to 1902;

SIR KENELM DIGBY, G.C.B., K.C., who was a County Court Judge from 1892 to 1894, and Permanent Under-Secretary of the Home Office from 1895 to 1903;

SIR ALFRED HOPKINSON, K.C., LL.D., represented Manchester and North Wiltshire in the House of Commons; was Principal of Owens College, Manchester, from 1898 to 1904; and Vice-Chancellor of Victoria University, Manchester, from 1900 to 1913;

MR. H. A. L. FISHER, Vice-Chancellor of the University of Sheffield;

MR. HAROLD COX, the well-known Journalist and Editor of the "Edinburgh Review," who represented Preston in the House of Commons from 1906 to 1910.

*How the Committee Worked.*

The Committee laboured for three months, examining the evidence, and more than 1,200 statements made by witnesses were considered. These depositions were in all cases taken down in this country by gentlemen of legal knowledge and experience, and the greatest care was exercised in the task.

*Doubt Removed as Work Proceeded.*

The Committee approached their responsible task in a spirit of doubt, but, to use their own words, "the further we went and the more evidence we examined, so much the more was our scepticism reduced.... When we found that things which had at first seemed improbable were testified to by many witnesses coming from different places, having had no communication with one another, and knowing nothing of one another's statements, the points in which they all agreed became more and more evidently true. And when this concurrence of testimony, this convergence upon what were substantially the same broad facts, showed itself in hundreds of depositions, **the truth of those broad facts stood out beyond question**."

*Fairness of Witnesses' Evidence.*

The Committee expected "to find much of the evidence coloured by passion, or prompted by an excited fancy. But they were impressed by the general moderation and matter-of-fact level-headedness of the witnesses."

*No desire to "Make a Case."*

Nor could the Committee, in examining the depositions, "detect the trace of any desire to 'make a case' against the German Army." "In one respect, the most weighty part of the evidence," according to the Committee, consisted of the diaries kept by the German soldiers themselves.

*A Terrible Record.*

The Report of the Committee, with the Appendix, covers 240 foolscap pages. These 240 pages of cold, judicial print make a terrible indictment against a so-called Civilised Power—and one, moreover, whose home is not in "Darkest Africa," but in the very heart of enlightened Europe.

In this pamphlet space will only permit of the insertion of the Findings of the Committee, and of some examples taken from the Report. *Those who seek fuller information should obtain one or other edition of the official Report and Appendix, particulars of which are given on the cover of this pamphlet.*

It should be borne in mind that this terrible record embraces a part only of the area in the occupation of German troops, and is based mainly on the statements of Belgian refugees *in this country*. If it had been possible to extend the enquiry, and to get evidence from the Belgians and the French now inhabiting the districts occupied by Germany, there is no doubt that the volume of evidence would have been much greater.

---

NOTE.—*For the purpose of this short pamphlet, the methodical arrangement in geographical areas followed in the Report has been abandoned, and a simpler grouping adopted. The whole of the language, however, in the following pages (apart from the headings) is the official language of the Report. In no instance has it been altered, except where an explanation is required, in which case the explanation is put in brackets. The references in the margin are to the pages in the report from which the statements have been taken. When taken from the Appendix, the letter "A" is prefixed.*

# 1. CIVILIANS MURDERED AND ILL-TREATED.

*The Care of the Belgian Civil Authorities to Collect Firearms from Civilians and to Warn them against taking part in the Hostilities.*

7

The Belgian King and Government were aware of the danger which would confront the civilian population of the country if it were tempted to take part in the work of national defence. Orders were accordingly issued by the civil governors of provinces, and by the burgomasters of towns, that the civilian inhabitants were to take no part in hostilities, and to offer no provocation to the invaders. That no excuse might be furnished for severities, the populations of many important towns were instructed to surrender all firearms into the hands of the local officials.

*The Kindness extended to the Invading Germans by the Civil Population of Belgium.*

26

Letters written to their homes, which have been found on the bodies of dead Germans, bear witness, in a way that now sounds pathetic, to the kindness with which they were received by the civil population. Their evident surprise at this reception was due to the stories which had been dinned into their ears of soldiers with their eyes gouged out, treacherous murders and poisoned food.

*Outbreak of Atrocities from the Moment the German Army crossed the Frontier.*

25

Murder, rape, arson and pillage began from the moment when the German Army crossed the frontier. For the first fortnight of the war, the towns and villages near Liège were the chief sufferers.... There is a certain significance in the fact that the outrages round Liège coincide with the unexpected resistance of the Belgian Army in that district, and that the slaughter which reigned from August 19th to the end of the month is contemporaneous with the period when the German Army's need for a quick passage through Belgium at all costs was deemed imperative.

> Article 46 of the Second International Peace Conference (Convention concerning the Laws and Customs of War on Land), held at the Hague in 1907, reads as follows:—
>
> *Family honour and rights, individual life, and private property, as well as religious convictions and worship, must be respected.*
>
> *Private property may not be confiscated.*

*Instances from Herve and Melen.*

**7**

"On the 4th of August," says one witness, "at Herve" (a village not far from the frontier), "I saw at about 2 o'clock in the afternoon, near the station, five Uhlans [German cavalry]; these were the first German troops I had seen. They were followed by a German officer and some soldiers in a motor car. The men in the car called out to a couple of young fellows who were standing about 30 yards away. The young men, being afraid, ran off, and then the Germans fired and killed one of them named D———." The murder of this innocent fugitive civilian was a prelude to the burning and pillage of Herve and of other villages in the neighbourhood, to the indiscriminate shooting of civilians of both sexes, and to the organised military execution of batches of selected males. Thus at Herve some 50 men escaping from the burning houses were seized, taken outside the town and shot. At Melen, a hamlet west of Herve, 40 men were shot. In one household alone the father and mother (names given) were shot, the daughter died after being outraged, and the son was wounded.

*The Slaughter of Civilians speedily became a Custom.*

The burning of the villages in this neighbourhood, and the wholesale slaughter of civilians, such as occurred at Herve, Micheroux and Soumagne appear to be connected with the exasperation caused by the resistance of Fort Fléron, whose guns barred the main road from Aix-la-Chapelle to Liège. Enraged by the losses which they had sustained, suspicious of the temper of the civilian population, and probably thinking that by exceptional severities at the outset they could cow the spirit of the Belgian nation, the German officers and men speedily accustomed themselves to the slaughter of civilians.

*No Official German Denial of Atrocities.*

**25**

Citizens of neutral states who visited Belgium in December and January report that the German authorities do not deny that non-combatants were systematically killed in large numbers during the first weeks of the invasion, and this, so far as we know, has never been officially denied.

*Flight of Belgian Refugees without Parallel.*

**25**

If it were denied, the flight and continued voluntary exile of thousands of Belgian refugees would go far to contradict a denial, for there is no historical parallel in modern times for the flight of a large part of a nation before an invader.

*German Government seek to justify Severities, but no Proof given of Alleged Firing by Civilians.*

> 25

The German Government have, however, sought to justify their severities on the grounds of military necessity, and have excused them as retaliation for cases in which civilians fired on German troops. There may have been cases in which such firing occurred, but no proof has ever been given, or, to our knowledge, attempted to be given, of such cases, nor of the allegations of shocking outrages perpetrated by Belgian men and women on German soldiers.

*On the contrary, Civilians were Warned after the Invasion.*

> 26

The inherent improbability of the German contention is shown by the fact that after the first few days of the invasion every possible precaution had been taken by the Belgian authorities, by way of placards and handbills, to warn the civilian population not to intervene in hostilities.

*Civilians Shot Indiscriminately and without any Inquiry.*

> 26

An invading army may be entitled to shoot at sight a civilian caught red-handed, or anyone who though not caught red-handed is proved guilty on inquiry. But this was not the practice followed by the German troops. They do not seem to have made any inquiry. They seized the civilians of the village indiscriminately and killed them, or such as they selected from among them, without the least regard to guilt or innocence. The mere cry "Civilisten haben geschossen" ("Civilians have been shooting") was enough to hand over a whole village or district, and even outlying places, to ruthless slaughter.

*Killing of Civilians on Scale without any Parallel in Modern Warfare between Civilised Powers.*

> 25

In the present war—and this is the gravest charge against the German Army—the evidence shows that the killing of non-combatants was carried out to an extent for which no previous war between nations claiming to be civilised furnishes any precedent.

*Mass of Evidence convinced Committee of its Truth.*

> 27

That these acts should have been perpetrated on the peaceful population of an unoffending country which was not at war with its invaders, but merely defending its own neutrality, guaranteed by the invading Power, may excite amazement and even incredulity. It was with amazement and almost with incredulity that the Committee first read the depositions relating to such acts. But when the evidence regarding Liège was followed by that regarding Aerschot, Louvain, Andenne, Dinant and the other towns and villages, the cumulative effect of such a mass of concurrent testimony became irresistible, and the Committee were driven to the conclusion that the things described had really happened.

*Killing of Civilians deliberately planned by the Higher Military Authorities and carried out methodically.*

> 27

The excesses recently committed in Belgium were, moreover, too widespread and too uniform in their character to be mere sporadic outbursts of passion or rapacity.

> 25

That this killing was done as part of a deliberate plan is clear from the facts set forth regarding Louvain, Aerschot, Dinant and other towns. The killing was done under orders in each place. It began at a certain fixed date, and stopped (with some few exceptions) at another fixed date.

*German Army Disciplined to Obey.*

> 27

The discipline of the German Army is proverbially stringent, and its obedience implicit.

> 23

It was to the discipline rather than the want of discipline in the Army that these outrages, which we are obliged to describe as systematic, were due, and the special official notices posted on certain houses that they were not to be destroyed show the fate which had been decreed for the others which were not so marked.

*A few German Officers showed Feelings of Humanity.*

> 27

The Committee gladly record the instances where the evidence shows that humanity had not wholly disappeared from some members of the German Army, and that they realised that the responsible heads of that organisation were employing them, not in war, but in butchery. "I am merely executing orders, and I should be shot if I did not execute them," said an officer to a witness at Louvain. At Brussels another officer said: "I have not done one hundredth part of what we have been ordered to do by the High German military authorities."

> 30

A humane German officer, witnessing the ruin of Aerschot, exclaimed in disgust: "I am a father myself, and I cannot bear this. It is not war, but butchery."

*Drink Responsible for many of the Worst Outrages.*

> 25

> 30

Many of the worst outrages appear to have been perpetrated by men under the influence of drink. Unfortunately, little seems to have been done to repress this source of danger.... Officers as well as men succumbed to the temptation of drink.

*The German Army is Responsible for Crimes which it did not Check.*

> 27

When an army is directed or permitted to kill non-combatants on a large scale, the ferocity of the worse natures springs into fuller life, and both lust and the thirst of blood become more widespread and more formidable. Had less licence been allowed to the soldiers, and had they not been set to work to slaughter civilians, there would have been fewer of those painful cases in which a depraved and morbid cruelty appears.

*The Taking and Murder of Hostages.*

> 27

Two classes of murders in particular require special mention, because one of them is almost new, and the other altogether unprecedented. The former is the seizure of peaceful citizens as so-called hostages to be kept as a pledge for the conduct of the civil population, or as a means to secure some military advantage, or to compel the payment of a contribution, the hostages being shot if the condition imposed by the arbitrary will of the invader is not fulfilled. Such hostage taking ... is opposed both to the rules of war and to every principle of justice and humanity.

*Murder in the Villages.*

> 27

The latter kind of murder is the killing of the innocent inhabitants of a village because shots have been fired, or are alleged to have been fired, on the troops by someone in the village. For this practice no previous example and no justification has been or can be pleaded.... In Belgium large bodies of men, sometimes including the burgomaster and the priest, were seized, marched by officers to a spot chosen for the purpose, and there shot in cold blood, without any attempt at trial or even enquiry, under the pretence of inflicting punishment upon the village, though these unhappy victims were not even charged with having themselves committed any wrongful act.

> 16

The Committee is specially impressed by the character of the outrages committed in the smaller villages.

*Aerschot and District* (August 25th).—Immediately after the battle of Malines ... a long series of murders were committed either just before or during the retreat of the army. Many of the inhabitants who were unarmed, including women and young children, were killed—some of them under revolting circumstances.

Evidence given goes to show that the death of these villagers was due, not to accident, but to deliberate purpose.

*A Death-stricken Area.*

> 14

The quadrangle of territory bounded by the towns of Aerschot, Malines, Vilvorde, and Louvain, is a rich agricultural tract, studded with small villages and comprising two considerable cities, Louvain and Malines. This district on August 19th passed into the hands of the Germans, and, owing perhaps to its proximity to Antwerp, then the seat of the Belgian Government and headquarters of the Belgian Army, it became from that date a scene of chronic outrage, with respect to which the Committee has received a great mass of evidence.

*Systematic Massacres.*

> 14

The arrival of the Germans in the district on August 19th was marked by systematic massacres and other outrages at Aerschot itself, Gelrode and some other villages.

*Sudden Outburst of Cruelty follows Belgian Victory.*

> 14

On August 25th the Belgians, sallying out of the defences of Antwerp, attacked the German positions at Malines, drove the enemy from the town and re-occupied many of the villages in the neighbourhood. And just as numerous outrages against the civilian population had been the immediate consequence of the temporary repulse of the German vanguard from Fort Fléron, so a large body of depositions testify to the fact that a sudden outburst of cruelty was the response of the German Army to the Belgian victory at Malines.

*A Reign of Terror.*

> 14

The battle of Malines ... was the occasion of numerous murders committed by the German Army in retreating through the villages of Sempst, Hofstade, Eppeghem, Elewyt and elsewhere. In the second place it led ... to the massacres, plunderings and burnings at Louvain, the signal for which was provided by shots exchanged between the German Army, retreating after its repulse at Malines, and some members of the German garrison of Louvain, who mistook their fellow countrymen for Belgians. Lastly, the encounter at Malines seems to have stung the Germans into establishing a reign of terror in so much of the district comprised in the quadrangle as remained in their power.

*Louvain Peacefully Occupied by Germans for Six Days.*

> 19

*Louvain and District.*—The events spoken to as having occurred in and around Louvain between August 19th and 25th deserve close attention.

For six days the Germans were in peaceful occupation of the city. No houses were set on fire—no citizens killed. There was a certain amount of looting of empty houses, but otherwise discipline was effectively maintained. The condition of Louvain during these days was one of relative peace and quietude, presenting a striking contrast to the previous and contemporaneous conduct of the German Army elsewhere.

*A Sudden Change—Murder of Civilians and Destruction of Property.*

19

On the evening of August 25th a sudden change took place. The Germans, on that day repulsed by the Belgians, had retreated to and re-occupied Louvain. Immediately the devastation of that city and the destruction by fire of its population began.

*Defeated Germans Revenge themselves on Civilians.*

19

The inference is irresistible that the Army as a whole wreaked its vengeance on the civilian population and the buildings of the city in revenge for the setback which the Belgian arms had inflicted on them. A subsidiary cause alleged was the assertion, often made before, that civilians had fired upon the German Army.

The depositions which relate to Louvain are numerous, and are believed by the Committee to present a true and fairly complete picture of the events of August 25th and 26th and subsequent days.

*Civilians did not Fire.*

19

The Committee find no grounds for thinking that the inhabitants fired upon the German Army on the evening of August 25th. Eye-witnesses worthy of credence detail exactly when, where and how the firing commenced. Such firing was by Germans on Germans. No impartial tribunal could, so the Committee think, come to any other conclusion.

*Harried Villagers.*

21

The massacre of civilians at Louvain was not confined to its citizens. Large crowds of people were brought into Louvain from the surrounding districts.... Of the hundreds of people taken from the various villages and brought to Louvain as prisoners, some were massacred there, others were forced to march along with citizens of Louvain through various places, some being ultimately sent on the 29th to the Belgian lines at Malines, others were taken in trucks to Cologne, others were released.

*A Calculated Policy of Cruelty.*

23

The Committee are driven to the conclusion that the harrying of the villages in the district, the burning of a large part of Louvain, the massacres there, the marching out of the prisoners, and the transport to Cologne—all done without enquiry as to whether the particular persons seized or killed had committed any wrongful act—were due to a calculated policy carried out scientifically and deliberately, not merely with the sanction but under the direction of higher military authorities, and were not due to any provocation or resistance by the civilian population.

*The Tragedy of Beautiful Dinant.*

13

Just outside the prison one witness saw three lines of bodies, which he recognised as being those of neighbours. They were nearly all dead, but he noticed movement in some of them. There were about 120 bodies.... Unarmed civilians were killed in masses at other places near the prison. About 90 bodies were seen lying on the top of one another in a grass square opposite the convent. They included many relatives of a witness.... It is stated that, beside the 90 corpses referred to above, 60 corpses of civilians were recovered from a hole in the brewery yard, and that 48 bodies of women and children were found in a garden.

The Committee have no reason to believe that the civilian population of Dinant gave any provocation, or that any other defence can be put forward to justify the treatment inflicted upon its citizens.

As regards this town and the advance of the German Army from Dinant to Rethel on the Aisne, a graphic account is given in the diary of a Saxon officer. This diary confirms what is clear from the evidence as a whole both as regards these and other districts—that civilians were constantly taken as prisoners, often dragged from their homes and shot under the direction of the authorities without any charge being made against them. An event of the kind is thus referred to in a diary entry: "Apparently 200 men were shot. There must have been some innocent men amongst them. In future we shall have to hold an enquiry as to their guilt instead of shooting them." The shooting of inhabitants—women and children as well as men—went on after the Germans had passed Dinant on their way into France.

FURTHER EXAMPLES OF THE TREATMENT OF CIVILIANS.

9

Entries in a German diary show that on August 19th the German soldiers gave themselves up to debauchery in the streets of Liège, and on the night of the 20th (Thursday) a massacre took place in the streets.... The Belgian witnesses vehemently deny that there had been any provocation given, some stating that many German soldiers were drunk, others giving evidence which indicates that the affair was planned beforehand. It is stated that at 5 o'clock in the evening, long before the shooting, a citizen was warned by a friendly German soldier not to go out that night.

Though the cause of the massacre is in dispute, the results are known with certainty.... Many inhabitants were burnt alive in their houses, their efforts to escape being prevented by rifle fire. Twenty people were shot while trying to escape, before the eyes of one of the witnesses.... Thirty-two civilians were killed on that day, the 21st, in the Place de l'Université alone.

---
20
---

*Louvain.*—On August 26th (Wednesday) massacre, fire and destruction went on.... Citizens were shot and others taken prisoners.

Soldiers went through the streets saying "Man hat geschossen." ("They have been shooting.") One soldier was seen going along shooting in the air.... Some citizens were shot on opening the doors, others in endeavouring to escape.

---
21
---

These prisoners [civilians] were practically without food from early morning on the 26th until midnight on the 29th. Of the corpses seen on the road some had their hands tied behind their backs, others were burnt, some had been killed by blows.

"I did not dare to look at the dead bodies in the street, there were so many of them."

---
23
---

"The officers were worse than the men.... We had had nothing to eat or drink since the evening of the day before. A few compassionate soldiers gave us water to drink, but no official took the trouble to see that we were fed."

---
24
---

*Louvain* (German soldier's diary—No. 32).—"180 inhabitants are stated to have been shot after they had dug their own graves."

---
11
---

*Surice.*—On August 24th and 25th massacres were carried out in which many persons belonging to the professional classes as well as others were killed.

> 11

*Namur* was entered on August 24th. The troops signalised their entry by firing on a crowd of 150 unarmed, unresisting civilians, 10 alone of whom escaped.... As the inhabitants fled from the burning houses they were shot by the German troops.

> 11

In *Tamines*, a large village on the Meuse between Namur and Charleroi, the advance guard of the German Army appeared in the first fortnight in August, and in this, as well as in other villages in the district, it is proved that a large number of civilians, among them aged people, women and children, were deliberately killed by the soldiers.

> 21

*Tirlemont.*—The prisoners, of whom there are said to have been thousands, were not allowed even to have water to drink, although there were streams on the way from which the soldiers drank. Witness was given some milk at a farm, but as she raised it to her lips it was taken away from her.

> 22

*Journeys from Louvain to Cologne.*—Some of the trucks were abominably filthy. Prisoners were not allowed to leave to obey the calls of nature.... They were, in all, eight days in the train, crowded and almost without food. Two of the men went mad.

> 23

*Termonde.*—About 70 prisoners ... were taken to Lebbeke, where there were in all 300 prisoners, and there they were locked up in the church for three days and with scarcely any food.

> 23

*Ermeton* (Diary No. 19).—The exact translation of the extract, grim in its brevity, is as follows: "August 24/14. We took about 1,000 prisoners; at least 500 were shot. The village was burnt because inhabitants had also shot. Two civilians were shot at once."

> 9

*Wandre* (Diary of German soldier—Eitel Anders).—"In one house a whole collection of weapons was found. The inhabitants without exception were brought out and shot. This shooting was heart-breaking, as they all knelt down and prayed; but that was no ground for mercy. A few shots rang out, and they fell back into the green grass and slept for ever."

> 10

*Andenne.*—Almost immediately, the slaughter of these inhabitants began, and continued for over two hours, and intermittently during the night. Machine guns were brought into play. The German troops were said to be for the most part drunk, and they certainly murdered and ravaged unchecked.

> 11

About 400 people lost their lives in this massacre.... Eight men belonging to one family were murdered. Another man was placed close to a machine gun, which was fired through him. His wife brought his body home on a wheelbarrow. The Germans broke into her house and ransacked it, and piled up all the eatables in a heap on the floor and relieved themselves upon it. A hair-dresser was murdered in his kitchen, where he was sitting with a child on each knee.

> 12

*Montigny-sur-Sambre.*—On the Monday morning 27 civilians from one parish alone were seen lying dead in the hospital.

> 12

At *Monceau-sur-Sambre*, on August 21st, a young man of 18 was shot in his garden. His father and brother were seized in their house and shot in the courtyard of a neighbouring country house. The son was shot first. The father was compelled to stand close to the feet of his son's corpse and to fix his eyes upon him while he himself was shot.

> 11

At *Temploux*, on August 23rd, a Professor of Modern Languages at the College of Namur was shot at his front door by a German officer. Before he died he asked the officer the reason for this brutality, and the officer replied that he had lost his temper because some civilians had fired upon the Germans as they entered the village. This allegation was not proved.... After the murder the house was burnt.

> 17

*Elewyt.*—A man's naked body was tied up to a ring in the wall in the backyard of a house. He was dead, and his corpse was mutilated in a manner too horrible to record. A woman's naked body was also found in a stable abutting on the same backyard.

---
24

---

Bombardier Wetzel, of the 2nd Mounted Battery, 1st Kurhessian Field Artillery Regiment, No. 11, records an incident which happened in French territory near Lille on October 11th: "We had no fight, but we caught about 20 men and shot them." By this time killing not in a fight would seem to have passed into a habit.

## 2. WOMEN MURDERED AND OUTRAGED.

> 30

From the very first women were not safe. At Liège women and children were chased about the street by soldiers. One witness gives a story, very circumstantial in its details, of how women were publicly raped in the market place of the city, five young German officers assisting.

> 11

*Tamines.*—A witness describes how he saw the public square littered with corpses, and after a search found those of his wife and child, a little girl of 7.

> 24

*Wetteren Hospital.*—At this hospital was an old woman of 80 completely transfixed by a bayonet.

> 17

*Sempst.*—Witness saw a girl of 17 dressed only in a chemise and in great distress. She alleged that she herself and other girls had been dragged into a field, stripped naked and violated, and that some of them had then been killed with the bayonet.

> 17

*Eppeghem.*—On August 25th a pregnant woman who had been wounded with a bayonet was discovered in the convent. She was dying.

> 19

*Louvain.*—"In the middle of the night I heard a knock at the outer door of the stable, which led into a little street, and heard a woman's voice crying for help. I opened the door, and just as I was going to let her in, a rifle shot fired from the street by a German soldier rang out and the woman fell dead at my feet."

> 21

The wife of a witness ... was separated from him, and she saw other ladies made to walk before the soldiers with their hands above their heads. One, an old lady of 85 (name given) was dragged from her cellar and taken with them to the station.

"I saw the corpses of some women in the street. I fell down, and a woman who had been shot fell on top of me.... One woman whom I saw lying dead in the street was a Miss —— about 35. I also saw the body of —— (a woman). She had been shot. I saw an officer pull her corpse underneath a wagon."

> 13

*Dinant.*—He found his wife lying on the floor in a room. She had bullet wounds in four places, but was alive, and told her husband to return to the children.

> 30

Sixty women and children were confined in the cellar of a convent from Sunday morning till the following Friday (August 28th), sleeping on the ground, for there were no beds, with nothing to drink during the whole period, and given no food until the Wednesday, "when somebody threw into the cellar two sticks of macaroni and a carrot for each prisoner."

> 16

In *Malines* itself many bodies were seen. One witness saw a German soldier cut a woman's breasts after he had murdered her, and saw many other dead bodies of women in the streets.

> 16

*Gelrode.*—A woman was shot by some German soldiers as she was walking home. This was done at a distance of 100 yards, and for no apparent reason.

> 17

*Hofstade.*—The corpse of a woman was seen at the blacksmith's. She had been killed with the bayonet.... Two young women were lying in the backyard of the house. One had her breasts cut off, the other had been stabbed.... In the garden of a house in the main street bodies of two women were observed.

> 30

*Campenhout* [Statement of a valet].—"One of the officers ... putting a revolver to my mistress' temple shot her dead. The officer was obviously drunk. The other officers continued to drink and sing, and they did not pay great attention to the killing of my mistress. The officer who shot my mistress then told my master to dig a grave and bury my mistress. My master and the officer went into the garden, the officer threatening my master with a pistol. My master was then forced to dig the grave, and to bury the body of my mistress in it. I cannot say for what reason they killed my mistress. The officer who did it was singing all the time."

# 3. THE MURDER AND ILL-TREATMENT OF CHILDREN.

> 32

There can be no possible defence for the murder of children.

> 33

Whether or no Belgian civilians fired on German soldiers, young children, at any rate, did not fire. The number and character of these murders constitute the most distressing feature connected with the conduct of the war so far as it is revealed in the depositions submitted to the Committee.

> 32

It is clearly shown that many offences were committed against infants and quite young children. On one occasion children were even roped together and used as a military screen against the enemy, on another three soldiers went into action carrying small children to protect themselves from flank fire.

> 18

At *Haecht* several children had been murdered; one of two or three years old was found nailed to the door of a farmhouse by its hands and feet, a crime which seems almost incredible, but the evidence for which we feel bound to accept. In the garden of this house was the body of a girl who had been shot in the forehead.

> 18

*Capelle-au-Bois.*—Two children were murdered in a cart, and their corpses were seen by many witnesses at different stages of the cart's journey.

> 11

*Tamines.*—One witness describes how she saw a Belgian boy of fifteen shot on the village green, and a day or two later on the same green a little girl and her two brothers (name given) who were looking at the German soldiers were killed before her eyes for no apparent reason.

> 17

*Boort Meerbeek.*—A German soldier was seen to fire three times at a little girl of five years old. Having failed to hit her, he subsequently bayoneted her. He was killed with the butt end of a rifle by a Belgian soldier who had seen him commit this murder from a distance.

> 17

*Weerde.*—Two children were killed in a village—apparently Weerde—quite wantonly as they were standing in the road with their mother. They were three or four years old, and were killed with the bayonet.

> 19

*Eppeghem.*—The dead body of a child of two was seen pinned to the ground with a German lance.

> 17

*Hofstade.*—On a side road ... was seen ... the dead body of a boy of five or six with his hands nearly severed.

> 33

In *Hofstade* and *Sempst*, in *Haecht*, *Rotselaar* and *Wespelaer*, many children were murdered.

> 21

*Louvain* (August 28th).—One woman went mad, some children died, others were born.... (August 29th, outside Louvain): Some corpses were those of children who had been shot.

> 30

*A small village.*—There were two little children—a boy about 4 or 5, and a girl of about 6 or 7. The boy's left hand was cut off at the wrist and the girl's right hand at the same place. They were both quite dead.

> 32

*Malines.*—"One day when the Germans were not actually bombarding the town, I left my house to go to my mother's house in High Street. My husband was with me. I saw eight German soldiers, and they were drunk. They were singing and making a lot of noise and dancing about. As the German soldiers came along the street I saw a small child, whether boy or girl I could not see, come out of a house. The child was about 2 years of age. The child came into the middle of the street so as to be in the way of the soldiers. The soldiers were walking in twos. The first line of two passed the child. One of the second line, the man on the left, stepped aside and drove his bayonet with both hands into the child's stomach, lifting the child into the air on his bayonet and carrying it away on his bayonet, he and his comrades still singing. The child screamed when the soldier struck it with his bayonet, but not afterwards."

# 4. BRUTAL TREATMENT OF THE AGED, THE CRIPPLED AND THE INFIRM.

> 11

At *Denée*, on August 28th, a Belgian soldier who had been taken prisoner saw three civilian fellow-prisoners shot. One was a cripple and another an old man of 80, who was paralysed. It was alleged by two German soldiers that these men had shot at them with rifles. Neither of them had rifles, nor had they anything in their pockets. The witness actually saw the Germans search them and nothing was found.

> 20

*Louvain.*—"Subsequently my master—an old gentleman—was bayoneted and shot."... Among other persons whose houses were burnt was an old man of 90, lying dangerously ill, who was taken out on his mattress and left lying in his garden all night. He died shortly after in the hospital.

> 18

The journey to Louvain is thus described by a witness: "We were all marched off to Louvain, walking. There were some very old people, amongst others a man 90 years of age. The very old people were drawn in carts and barrows by the younger men. There was an officer with a bicycle, who shouted, as people fell out by the side of the road, 'Shoot them.'"

> 8

At *Heure le Romain* ... some bedridden old men were imprisoned in the church.

> 11

*Andenne.*—A paralytic was murdered in his garden.

> 29

*Beaumetz.*—They saw two old men—between 60 and 70 years of age—and one old woman lying close to each other in the garden. All three had the scalps cut right through.... They were still bleeding.

# 5. THE USE OF CIVILIANS AS SCREENS.

> 33

The Committee had before them a considerable body of evidence with reference to the practice of the Germans of using civilians and sometimes military prisoners as screens from behind which they could fire upon the Belgian troops, in the hope that the Belgians would not return the fire for fear of killing or wounding their own fellow-countrymen.

> 31

The use of women and even children as a screen for the protection of the German troops is referred to.... From the number of troops concerned, it must have been commanded or acquiesced in by officers, and in some cases the presence and connivance of officers is proved.

> 23

*Termonde.*—Two hundred civilians were utilised as a screen by the German troops.

> 24

*Binnenstraat.*—The civilians were utilised on Saturday, the 26th September, as a screen.

> 33

*Mons.*—On August 24th men, women and children were actually pushed into the front of the German position outside Mons. The witness speaks of 16 to 20 women, about a dozen children and half a dozen men being there.

> 34

At *Tournai* 400 Belgian civilians—men, women and children—were placed in front of the Germans, who then engaged the French.

> 34

At *Ypres* the Germans drove women in front of them by pricking them with bayonets. The wounds were afterwards seen by the witness.

> 34

At *Londerzeel* 30 or 40 civilians—men, women and children—were placed at the head of a German column.

One witness from *Termonde* was made to stand in front of the Germans, together with others, all with their hands above their heads. Those who allowed their hands to drop were at once prodded with the bayonet.

# 6. THE KILLING OF WOUNDED SOLDIERS AND PRISONERS.

> 35

After making all allowances, there remain certain instances in which it is clear that quarter was refused to persons desiring to surrender when it ought to have been given, or that persons already so wounded as to be incapable of fighting further, were wantonly shot or bayoneted.

> 36

In one case, given very circumstantially, a witness [a British lance-corporal, whose evidence has been confirmed by a lieutenant and a private] tells how a party of wounded British soldiers were left in a chalk pit, all very badly hurt, and quite unable to make resistance. One of them, an officer, held up his handkerchief as a white flag, and this "attracted the attention of a party of about eight Germans. The Germans came to the edge of the pit. It was getting dusk, but the light was still good, and everything clearly discernible. One of them, who appeared to be carrying no arms, and who, at any rate, had no rifle, came a few feet down the slope into the chalk pit, within eight or ten yards of some of the wounded men." He looked at the men, laughed, and said something in German to the Germans who were waiting on the edge of the pit. Immediately one of them fired at the officer, then three or four of these 10 soldiers were shot, then another officer, and the witness, and the rest of them. "After an interval of some time I sat up and found that I was the only man of the 10 who were living when the Germans came into the pit remaining alive, and that all the rest were dead."

# 7. LOOTING, BURNING AND DESTRUCTION OF PROPERTY.

> 34

There is an overwhelming mass of evidence of the deliberate destruction of private property by the German soldiers. The destruction, in most cases, was effected by fire, and the German troops had been provided beforehand with appliances for rapidly setting fire to houses. Among the appliances enumerated by witnesses are syringes for squirting petrol, guns for throwing small inflammable bombs, and small pellets made of inflammable material. Specimens of the last-mentioned have been shown to members of the Committee. Besides burning houses the Germans frequently smashed furniture and pictures; they also broke in doors and windows. Frequently, too, they defiled houses by relieving the wants of nature upon the floor. They also appear to have perpetrated the same vileness upon piled up heaps of provisions, so as to destroy what they could not themselves consume.

> 25

Villages, even large parts of a city, were given to the flames as part of the terrorising policy.

> 35

The general conclusion is that the burning and destruction of property which took place was only in a very small minority of cases justified by military necessity.

> 19

*Louvain.*—Then the corps of incendiaries got to work. They had broad belts with the words "Gott mit uns" ("God with us"), and their equipment consisted of a hatchet, a syringe, a small shovel and a revolver. Fires blazed up in the direction of the Law Courts and St. Martin's Barracks.

> 19

A witness: "When we got to the Place de la Station ... not a single house in the place was standing."

> 20

On the 26th (Wednesday), in the city of Louvain, massacre, fire, and destruction went on. The University, with its Library, the Church of St. Peter, and many houses were set on fire and burnt to the ground.

> 12

*Tamines.*—A witness went there on August 27th and says: "It is absolutely destroyed and a mass of ruins."

> 9

*Liège.*—The Rue des Pitteurs and houses in the Place de l'Université and the Quai des Pêcheurs were systematically fired with benzine.

> 16

*Aerschot.*—The houses were set on fire with special apparatus.

> 12

*Montigny-sur-Sambre.*—Incendiaries, with a distinctive badge on their arm, went down the main street throwing handfuls of inflammatory and explosive pastilles into the houses. These pastilles were carried by them in bags, and in this way about 130 houses were destroyed in the main street.

> 11

*Namur.*—A witness of good standing ... describes how the town was set on fire systematically in six different places.... Not less than 140 houses were burnt. On the 25th the hospital was set on fire with inflammable pastilles, the pretext being that soldiers in the hospital had fired upon the Germans.

> 13

*Dinant.*—The town was systematically set on fire by hand grenades.... The houses and villages were pillaged and property wantonly destroyed.

> 12

At *Morlanwelz*, about this time, the British Army, together with some French cavalry, were compelled to retire before the German troops. The latter took the burgomaster and his manservant prisoner and shot them both in front of the Hotel de Ville at Péronne (Belgium), where the bodies were left in the street for 48 hours. They burnt the Hotel de Ville and 62 houses. The usual accusation of firing by civilians was made. It is strenuously denied by the witness, who declares that three or four days before the arrival of the Germans, circulars had been distributed to every house and placards had been posted in the town ordering the deposit of all firearms at the Hotel de Ville, and that this order had been complied with.

> 24

*Erpe.*—The village was deliberately burnt.

> 23

*Termonde.*—The town was partially burnt. One witness was taken prisoner in the street by some German soldiers, together with several other civilians. At about 12 o'clock on the 5th some of the tallest and strongest men amongst the prisoners were picked out to go round the streets with paraffin. Three or four carts containing paraffin tanks were brought up, and a syringe was used to put paraffin on to the houses, which were then fired. The process of destruction began with the houses of rich people, and afterwards the houses of the poorer classes were treated in the same manner.

> 8

*Herve.*—From the 8th to the 10th over 300 houses were burnt.

> 8

*Visé.*—On or about the 14th and 15th the village was completely destroyed. Officers directed the incendiaries, who worked methodically with benzine.

> 9

*Diary of Eitel Anders*, a German soldier.—"We crossed the Belgian frontier on August 15th, 1914, at 11.50 in the forenoon, and then we went steadily along the main road till we got into Belgium. Hardly were we there when we had a horrible sight. Houses were burnt down.... Not one of the hundreds of houses were spared. Everything was plundered and burnt."

> 24

*Diary of Mathern, of the 4th Company of Jägers*, states that at a village between Birnal and Dinant, on Sunday, August 23rd, "about 220 inhabitants were shot, and the village was burnt.... All villages, chateaux and houses are burnt down during the night. It is a beautiful sight to see the fires all round us in the distance."

*Looting.*

> 34

The German troops, both in Belgium and France, are proved to have been guilty of persistent looting. In the majority of cases the looting took place from houses, but there is also evidence that German soldiers, and even officers, robbed their prisoners, both civil and military, of sums of money and other portable possessions. It was apparently well known throughout the German Army that towns and villages would be burned whenever it appeared that any civilians had fired upon the German troops, and there is reason to suspect that this known intention of the German military authorities in some cases explains the sequence of events which led up to the burning and sacking of a town or village. The soldiers, knowing that they would have an opportunity of plunder if the place was condemned, had a motive for arranging some incident which would provide the necessary excuse for condemnation. More than one witness alleges that shots coming from the window of a house were fired by German soldiers, who had forced their way into the house for the purpose of thus creating an alarm.

---
15
---

*Aerschot.*—Throughout the day the town was looted by the soldiers.

---
8
---

*Visé.*—Antiques and china were removed from the houses before their destruction by officers who guarded the plunder, revolver in hand.

---
A 171
---

Translated extract from diary of Stephan Luther: "We live like God in France."

---
A 181
---

Translated extracts from the field notebook of an officer in the 178th Regiment, XIIth (Saxon) Corps: "August 17th.—In the afternoon I had a look at the little chateau belonging to one of the King's Secretaries (not at home). Our men had behaved like regular vandals. They had looted the cellar first.... Everything was topsy-turvy—magnificent furniture, silk, and even china.... I am sure they must have taken away a heap of useless stuff simply for the pleasure of looting."

---
A 182
---

"September 3rd.—Still at Rethel, ... the houses are charming inside. The middle class in France has magnificent furniture.... Every bit of furniture broken, mirrors smashed. The Vandals themselves could not have done more damage. This place is a disgrace to our army."

"I could not resist taking a little memento myself here and there."

Article 47 of the Second International Peace Conference (Convention concerning the Laws and Customs of War on Land), held at the Hague in 1907, reads as follows:—

*Pillage is expressly forbidden.*

# FINDINGS OF THE COMMITTEE.

37

"The Committee have come to a definite conclusion upon each of the heads under which the evidence has been classified.

"It is proved:—

"(i) That there were in many parts of Belgium deliberate and systematically organised massacres of the civil population, accompanied by many isolated murders and other outrages.

"(ii) That in the conduct of the war generally innocent civilians, both men and women, were murdered in large numbers, women violated, and children murdered.

"(iii) That looting, house burning, and the wanton destruction of property were ordered and countenanced by the officers of the German Army, that elaborate provision had been made for systematic incendiarism at the very outbreak of the war, and that the burnings and destruction were frequent where no military necessity could be alleged, being indeed part of a system of general terrorization.

"(iv) That the rules and usages of war were frequently broken, particularly by the using of civilians, including women and children, as a shield for advancing forces exposed to fire, to a less degree by killing the wounded and prisoners, and in the frequent abuse of the Red Cross and the White Flag.

"Sensible as they are of the gravity of these conclusions, the Committee conceive that they would be doing less than their duty if they failed to record them as fully established by the evidence. **Murder, lust, and pillage prevailed over many parts of Belgium on a scale unparalleled in any war between civilised nations during the last three centuries.**

"Our function is ended when we have stated what the evidence establishes, but we may be permitted to express our belief that these disclosures will not have been made in vain if they touch and rouse the conscience of mankind, and we venture to hope that, as soon as the present war is over, the nations of the world in council will consider what means can be provided and sanctions devised to prevent the recurrence of such horrors as our generation is now witnessing."

---

Is YOUR conscience roused? Won't YOU take the most effective way of showing it—if you are a man under 40 and fit? The only way to put a stop to these and other crimes is to crush the German Army.

YOU can help either by joining the Army or by making munitions. Place YOUR services at the disposal of the military authorities.

If YOU are a woman, cannot you help a man to decide?

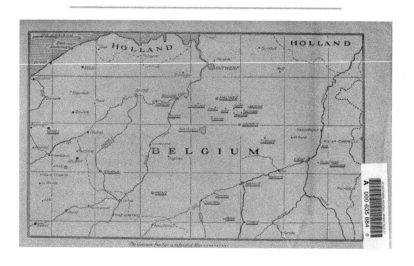